CLUE BO

Freshwater Animals

Gwen Allen   Joan Denslow

OXFORD UNIVERSITY PRESS

Oxford University Press, Great Clarendon Street, Oxford OX2 6DP

Oxford   New York
Athens Auckland Bangkok Bogotá Bombay
Buenos Aires Calcutta Cape Town Dar es Salaam
Delhi Florence Hong Kong Istanbul Karachi
Kuala Lumpur Madras Madrid Melbourne
Mexico City Nairobi Paris Singapore
Taipei Tokyo Toronto

and associated companies in
Berlin Ibadan

Oxford is a trade mark of Oxford University Press

© Oxford University Press 1997
First published 1970
New edition 1997

CLUE BOOKS - FRESHWATER ANIMALS
produced for Oxford University Press
by Bender Richardson White, Uxbridge

Editors: Lionel Bender, John Stidworthy Design: Ben White
Media Conversion and Page Make-up: MW Graphics
Project Manager: Kim Richardson
Original artwork: Derek Whiteley
Additional artwork: Ron Hayward

A CIP catalogue record for this book is available from the British Library

ISBN 0-19-910178-7 (hardback)   ISBN 0-19-910184-1 (paperback)

1 3 5 7 9 10 8 6 4 2

Printed in Italy

CONTENTS

ABOUT THIS BOOK

This book allows you to identify the most common freshwater animals of northern and western Europe. It is divided into three main sections: Introduction, Clues and Identification.

The Introduction section tells you about the lifestyles and habits of freshwater animals. It also tells you the best places and times to look for freshwater animals, and how to catch them to study them in more detail. When you have looked at the living animals, be sure to put them back where you found them.

The Clues section allows you to identify each animal you have found. Start on page 12 and follow the clues. The arrows and numbers in the right-hand margin tell you which page to go to next.

The Identification Section consists of information about each major group of freshwater animals and double-page colour plates illustrating the individual types or species. Most of the animals you find will be illustrated in this section. Alongside each illustration is a basic description of the animal. Measurements are given in millimetres or centimetres - abbreviated to mm or cm (1 cm = 10 mm = 2/5th inch). On colour plates starting on page 42, animals and the stages in their life cycles are drawn to the same scale. Alongside some illustrations is a black line showing the real size of that animal.

The coloured band at the top of each double-page spread helps you locate the relevant sections of the book: *blue* for Introduction, *yellow* for Clues, *red* for Identification. An arrowhead at the top right of a page or spread shows the topic continues on to the next page or spread. A bar at the top right indicates the end of that topic.

This is a book about animals that spend all or part of their lives in fresh water, in lakes, ponds, rivers and streams. The animals can be found under stones by the water's edge, on leaves and stems of plants, or swimming in the water.

In order to use this book you will need real animals. The illustrations below show the kinds of nets you will need when you are collecting them. Polythene bags in cartons or plastic buckets are useful for carrying the animals.

The best time to look for freshwater animals is in the spring and summer, when water plants are growing fastest and flowering, and animals are emerging from their winter slumber, mating and producing young.

When you have finished observations on the animals in your temporary aquarium, return them to the place where you found them, or to somewhere like it.

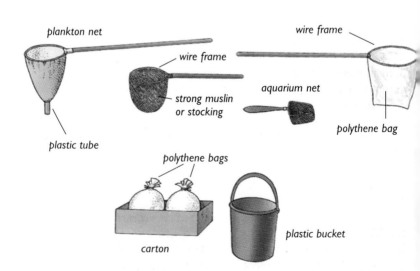

plankton net

wire frame

wire frame

strong muslin or stocking

aquarium net

polythene bag

plastic tube

polythene bags

plastic bucket

carton

You can find out in which particular part of the water your animals prefer to live by drawing a map of the area in which you are collecting, and plotting on it the places where you found the animals (see below).

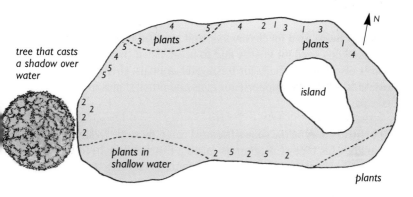

tree that casts a shadow over water

plants

plants

island

plants in shallow water

plants

N

l Lesser Water Boatman   2 Water fleas   3 Mayfly nymphs   4 tadpoles
5 fish seen resting nose to bank after dark

You can work out whether the animals are found:
1. in different places at different times of the day
2. in different places at different times of the year
3. in sunlight or shadow
4. in places where plants are growing or in open water
5. in the warmer or colder parts of the water.

What other things can you find out about the way the animals behave in a pond?

SAFETY
Take care when you are near ponds, lakes, rivers and streams. Do not go into the water if you cannot swim, and beware of strong currents.

All animals need food in order to grow. Some animals eat plants; they are called **HERBIVORES**. Others eat other animals; they are called **CARNIVORES**. Animals called **SCAVENGERS** eat dead plants and animals.

Plants provide food for herbivores, and produce the oxygen that all living things need for energy and to break down their food. Water plants also provide shade for freshwater animals, shelter from their enemies, and act as supports for eggs and other stages in the life cycle (see pages 10–11)

The illustration below shows the food eaten by some freshwater animals. This type of diagram is called a **FOOD WEB**. In terms of numbers of individuals, there are far more herbivores than there are carnivores in the food web.

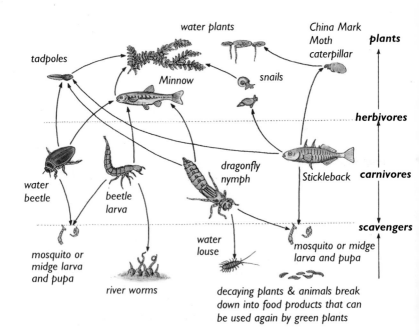

BREATHING

Animals that live in water either take oxygen from the water when they breathe, or rise to the surface to collect air. Watch your animals to see which they do.

When animals breathe they take in oxygen and get rid of carbon dioxide. Oxygen combines with digested food in muscles, bone and nerves to provide energy for movement and growth. The food is changed into carbon dioxide and water which are breathed out.

Fish, tadpoles and snails breathe through gills. These gills have capillaries (very small blood vessels) in them. They are called **VASCULAR GILLS**. Blood flows through the capillaries and collects oxygen from the water. If you look at the gills of a tadpole under a microscope, you can see the blood moving through the capillaries.

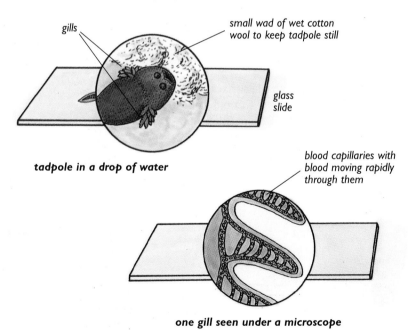

gills

small wad of wet cotton wool to keep tadpole still

glass slide

tadpole in a drop of water

blood capillaries with blood moving rapidly through them

one gill seen under a microscope

Insects have different gills called
TRACHEAL GILLS. These have air tubes
which collect oxygen from the water.

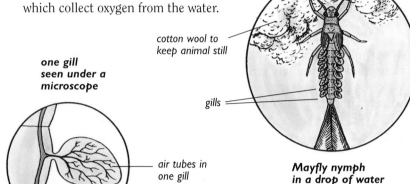

**one gill
seen under a
microscope**

cotton wool to
keep animal still

gills

air tubes in
one gill

**Mayfly nymph
in a drop of water**

**inside of an insect
showing the
spiracles and some
of the air tubes
inside the body**

Some animals come to the surface to
breathe air. Some breathe through tubes
in their tail filaments. Others collect air
as a bubble over their hairy bodies; it
passes into air tubes in the body
through holes called **SPIRACLES.**

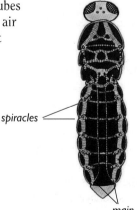

spiracles

main air tubes

MOVING

Many animals swim; they push against the water in order to move forward. Watch the animals you have found to see how they push against the water.

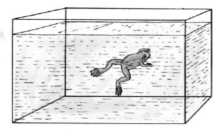

frog pushing against the water with webbed feet

Many animals have streamlined bodies in order to move easily through the water.

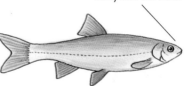

pointed front cuts easily into the water

Which of your animals are streamlined? Watch a fish using its fins and tail to change direction as it swims. How does it do this?

Pond skaters and other animals move about on the surface of the water; snails often glide along underneath the surface. Some pond animals seem to float to the top unless they swim hard or cling to plants to keep themselves down. Which ones behave in this way? Do these animals have a bubble of air around their bodies?

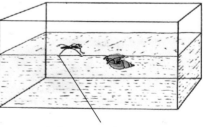

hollows where feet press on the surface of the water

All animals that live in fresh water hatch from eggs (see page 20).

Some eggs hatch into young that do not at first look like their parents; at this stage of their life they are called LARVAE (see page 13).

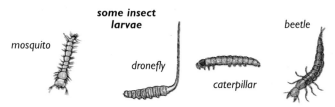

some insect larvae

mosquito

dronefly

caterpillar

beetle

Larvae of frogs, toads and newts are called TADPOLES (see page 77). Insect larvae eat a great deal of food and grow quickly; they shed their skins (moult) every time they grow too big for them. When the insect larva is fully grown it stops eating and changes into a PUPA. The pupa does not move; it has a hard, protective skin. Within this skin, it changes into an adult.

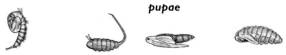

pupae

When the change is complete the pupal skin bursts and the adult insect emerges.

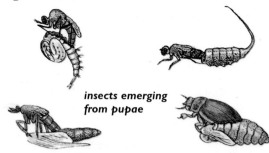

insects emerging from pupae

Tadpoles do not turn into pupae: instead, they gradually change into adults.

Some insect eggs hatch into young that look like their parents, but their wings are not fully grown. These animals are called NYMPHS; they eat a great deal of food and moult when they grow too big for their skins. Each time they moult their wings can be seen to be larger.

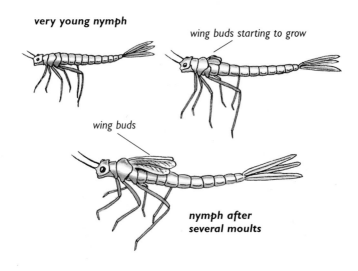

very young nymph

wing buds starting to grow

wing buds

nymph after several moults

The eggs of all other freshwater animals hatch into young that look like small versions of their parents.

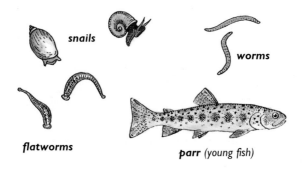

snails

worms

flatworms

parr (young fish)

The clues on pages 12–39 will help you to name the animals you collect. Begin by using the clues on pages 12 to 15.

Look carefully at each animal. If it is small, use a magnifying lens or microscope. Find the clue that fits it, then turn to the page given for the next clue. Repeat this until you find its name or group.

Most of the drawings of small animals and parts of animals in the clues are larger than life-size.

CLUE A

If the animal has four legs and hairless skin without scales, it is an **AMPHIBIAN**.

 76

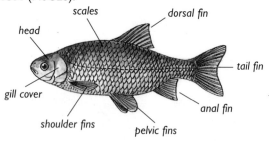

CLUE B

If the animal has fins and usually a scaly skin, it is a **FISH** (PISCES). 36

scales

dorsal fin

head

tail fin

gill cover

anal fin

shoulder fins

pelvic fins

CLUE C

If the animal has six jointed legs, three parts to its body (head, thorax, abdomen) and wings, it is an adult **INSECT**.

26

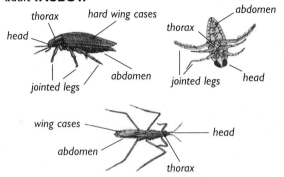

thorax *hard wing cases* *abdomen*

head *thorax*

jointed legs *abdomen* *jointed legs* *head*

wing cases *head*

abdomen

thorax

CLUE D

If the animal has six jointed legs and wing buds, it is a young **INSECT NYMPH**.

27

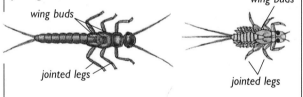

wing buds

wing buds

jointed legs

jointed legs

CLUE E

If the animal has six jointed legs, but no wings or wing buds, it is probably an **INSECT LARVA**

30

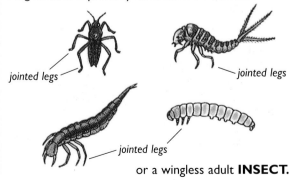

jointed legs

jointed legs

jointed legs

or a wingless adult **INSECT**.

41

CLUE F If the animal has eight jointed legs, only one or two parts to its body and no wings, it belongs to the **ARACHNIDS** (spiders and mites). 33

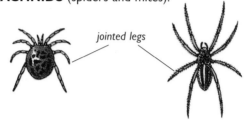

jointed legs

CLUE G If the animal has ten or more jointed legs but no wings, it belongs to the **CRUSTACEANS** (crab group). 34

jointed legs   *jointed legs*

CLUE H If the animals are very small (3mm or less), transparent, move quickly and have legs that can be seen only if looked at under good magnification, they are **WATER FLEAS,** belonging to the **CRUSTACEANS** (crab group). 60

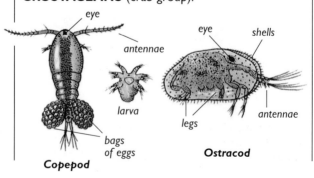

eye

antennae

eye   *shells*

larva

legs   *antennae*

bags of eggs

Copepod   **Ostracod**

CLUE H continued

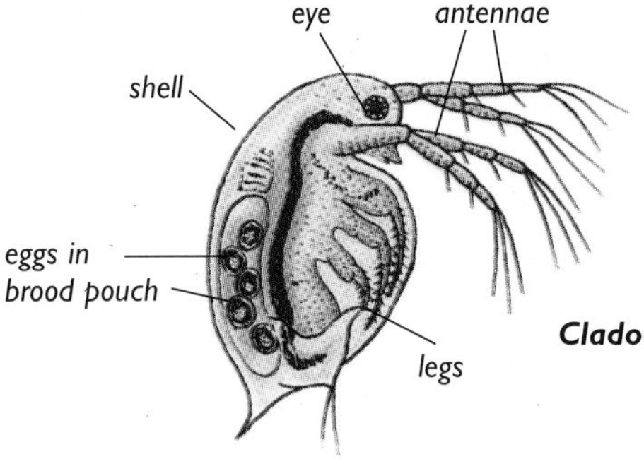
eye
antennae
shell
eggs in
brood pouch
legs

Cladoceran

If the animals are like water fleas but larger (about 20mm) they may be **FAIRY SHRIMPS.**

35 E

CLUE I

If the animal has no legs or wings and has a solid shell it is a **MOLLUSC.**

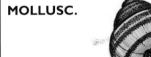

16 A

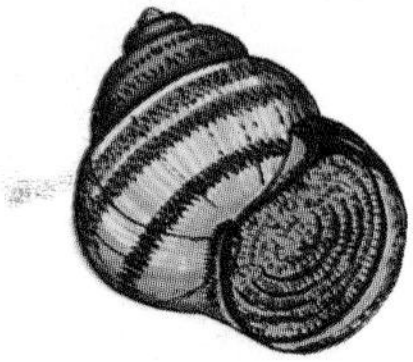

CLUE J

If the animal has no legs or wings and is not less than 1 cm long

16 B, 17 C–E

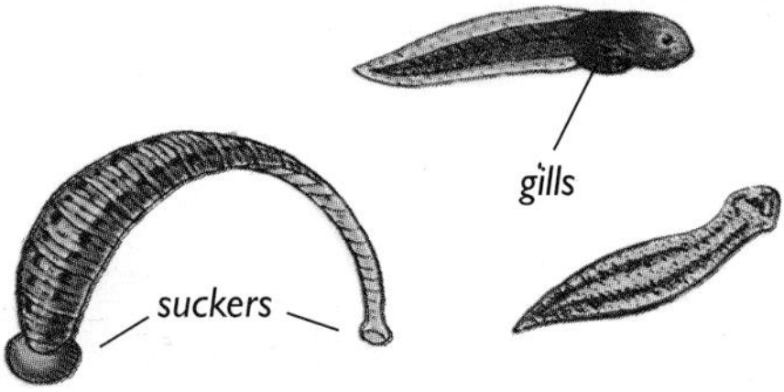
gills
suckers

CLUE K

If the animal does not look like any of these, examine it carefully, using a strong lens or microscope if necessary.

18

CLUE A | If the animal has one solid shell

 24 B

If the animal has two shells

hinge

 24 A

CLUE B | If the animal looks like this, it is probably a **TADPOLE**.

 77

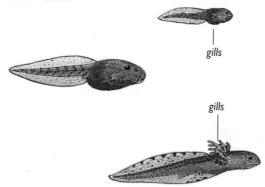

gills

gills

CLUE C | If the animal has a sucker at each end of its body, it is a **LEECH**. 63

suckers

CLUE D | If the animal looks like this, it is a **RAT-TAILED MAGGOT**, the **LARVA** of a **DRONEFLY**. 53

tail

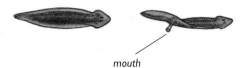

CLUE E | If the animal has a smooth, flattened body, and glides over hard surfaces, it is a **FLATWORM**. 65

mouth

CLUE A | If the animal has a body made up of rings (segments) with groups of bristles at its head or tail end, and has jerky, wriggling movements, it may be a **MOSQUITO** (sometimes called a Gnat) or **MIDGE LARVA**.
If the animal looks like this but does not move jerkily, it is probably a **BLACKFLY LARVA**.

54
5

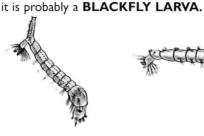

If the animal has a large head and looks like this, it is a **MOSQUITO** or **MIDGE PUPA**.

5

CLUE B | If the animal has a body made up of rings (segments) with very short bristles on each ring, it is a **WORM**.

6

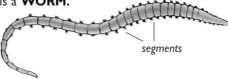

segments

CLUE C | If the animal has tentacles on one end of its body, it is a **HYDRA**.

6

tentacles with stings for catching prey

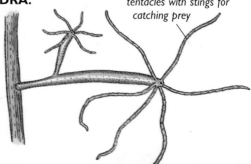

CLUE D

If the animal is minute and looks like this, it may be a **WHEEL-ANIMAL** or **ROTIFER**.

 65

wheel-like rings of very thin thread

CLUE E

If the animals are minute and colourless, they belong to a group of very simple animals called **PROTOZOA**.

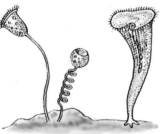

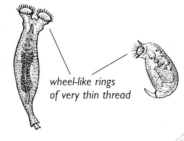

some kinds of protozoa

If you want to know more about these animals you will need to look at other books (see page 80).

CLUE F

If it does not look like any of these, it may be **EGGS**.

 20

EGGS

If you look at the eggs of many freshwater animals
under magnification, you will be able to see, inside
the eggs, animals at different stages of development
(see page 77). If you find eggs like the ones
illustrated on these pages, turn to the page number
by the drawing.

CLUE A   Eggs surrounded by jelly, floating in the water

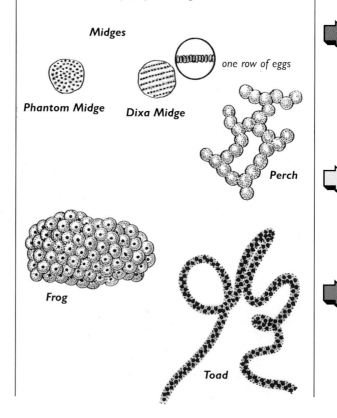

Midges

Phantom Midge   *Dixa Midge*   one row of eggs

Perch

Frog

Toad

5·

3·

7·

CLUE B | Eggs surrounded by jelly attached to plants and stones

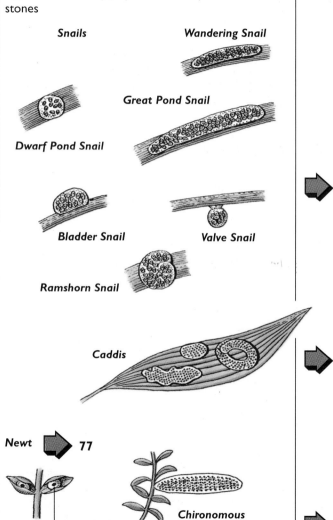

Snails

Wandering Snail

Great Pond Snail

Dwarf Pond Snail

66

Bladder Snail

Valve Snail

Ramshorn Snail

Caddis

52

Newt 77

eggs wrapped in leaf

Chironomous Midge

55

CLUE A | Eggs floating on water

Mosquito ➡ 54

float

one egg

Gnat raft ➡ 54

one egg

lid

Dragonfly ➡ 48

Mayfly ➡ 49

Dronefly ➡ 53

CLUE B | Eggs laid at the bottom of a pond or stream

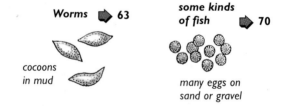

Worms ➡ 63

some kinds of fish ➡ 70

cocoons in mud

many eggs on sand or gravel

CLUE C | Eggs laid inside plant stems

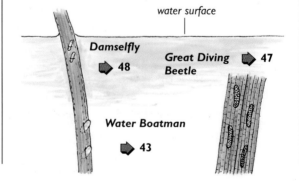

water surface

Damselfly ➡ 48

Great Diving Beetle ➡ 47

Water Boatman ➡ 43

CLUE D Eggs laid on plants above the water

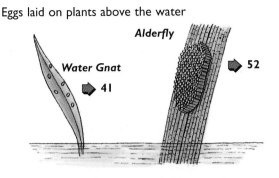

Alderfly ➡ 52

Water Gnat ➡ 41

CLUE E Eggs laid on plant stems or stones in the water

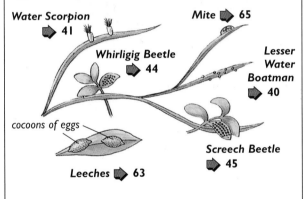

Water Scorpion ➡ 41

Mite ➡ 65

Whirligig Beetle ➡ 44

Lesser Water Boatman ➡ 40

cocoons of eggs

Screech Beetle ➡ 45

Leeches ➡ 63

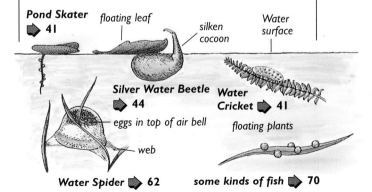

Pond Skater ➡ 41

floating leaf

silken cocoon

Water surface

Silver Water Beetle ➡ 44

Water Cricket ➡ 41

eggs in top of air bell

floating plants

web

Water Spider ➡ 62

some kinds of fish ➡ 70

For general information on animals with shells, see
pages 66–67.

CLUE A

If the shell is large, dark, and looks like this, it is a
FRESHWATER MUSSEL.

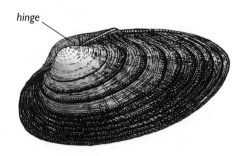

hinge

If the shell is small, pale and
looks like this, it is a **PEA** or
ORB COCKLE.

CLUE B

If the shell is a flat coil, it is
a **RAMSHORN SNAIL.**

If the shell is pointed

25
C

CLUE C

If the shell is brown with the opening to the right, and the tentacles are small with the eyes at the base, it is probably a **POND SNAIL**.

 68, 69

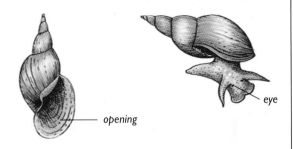

eye

opening

If it looks like this, has an opening to the left, and is very shiny, it is probably a **BLADDER SNAIL**.

 68

opening

If there is a shell-like plate (operculum) on its foot, it is a **FRESHWATER WINKLE** or **VALVE SNAIL**.

 68, 69

operculum

young winkle emerging

Look carefully at the hard wing cases.

CLUE A

If the animal has hard wing cases and a shield-like part (scutellum) on its back, it is one of the **BUGS.**

 40

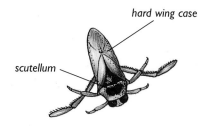

hard wing case

scutellum

CLUE B

If the hard wing cases cover most of the animal's body, it is one of the **BEETLES.**

 44

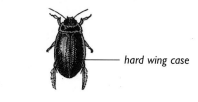

hard wing case

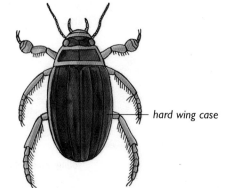

hard wing case

Using a magnifying lens look carefully at the animal.

CLUE A

If the animal has leaf-like gills along the sides of its body and three tail filaments, it is probably a **MAYFLY NYMPH.**

 49

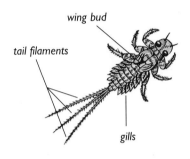

wing bud

tail filaments

gills

CLUE B

If the animal has a slender body, three tail filaments, very large eyes and jaws on the end of a 'mask', it is probably a **DAMSELFLY NYMPH.** (Look at the Dragonfly nymph on page 28 to see what a mask is.)

 48

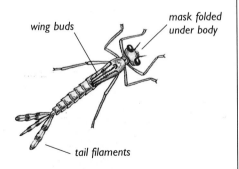

mask folded under body

wing buds

tail filaments

CLUE C | If the animal has a slender body, two tail filaments and long antennae, it is probably a **STONEFLY NYMPH**.

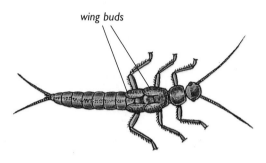

wing buds

CLUE D | If the animal has a stout body, very large eyes and jaws on the end of a mask, it is probably a **DRAGONFLY NYMPH**.

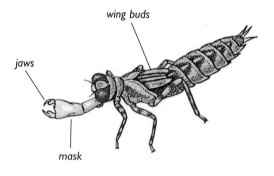

wing buds

jaws

mask

CLUE E

If the animal's hind legs are longer than the others, and are used for swimming, it may be a **WATER BOATMAN NYMPH.**

 40

wing buds

CLUE F

If the animal is small, has long legs and moves quickly over the surface of the water, it may be a **POND SKATER, WATER CRICKET** or **WATER GNAT.**

 41

CLUE A | If the animal has jointed gills along the sides of its body, it is probably an **ALDERFLY LARVA.**

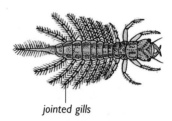

jointed gills

CLUE B | If the animal has gills along the sides of its body and four tail filaments, it may be a **WHIRLIGIG BEETLE LARVA.**

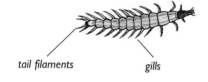

tail filaments   *gills*

CLUE C | If the animal has three tail filaments and looks like this, it is probably a **SCREECH BEETLE LARVA.**

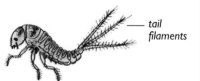

tail filaments

44

CLUE D

If the animal has a long body, large biting jaws and two short tail filaments, it is probably a **WATER BEETLE LARVA.**

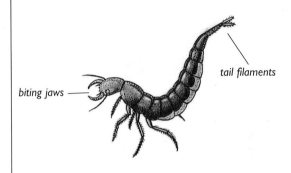

tail filaments

biting jaws

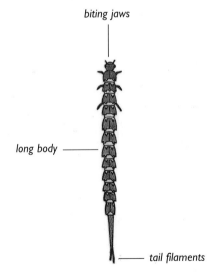

biting jaws

long body

tail filaments

CLUE E

If the animal lives in a tube made of leaves, sticks or stones, it is a **CADDIS LARVA.**

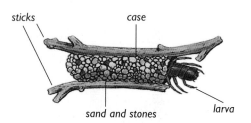

5

sticks   case

sand and stones   larva

case   larva

spirally arranged plant pieces

CLUE F

If the animal is a caterpillar, and lives in a tube of silk attached to the underside of a floating leaf, it is a **CHINA MARK MOTH LARVA.**

53

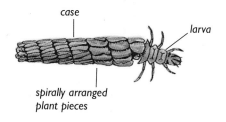

caterpillar

two pieces of leaf bound by silk

caterpillar

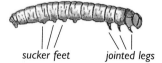

sucker feet   jointed legs

LUE A

If the animal has two parts to its body, with its legs attached to the front part, it is a **SPIDER**.

 62

LUE B

If the animal is very small (less than 5 mm), swims quickly, appears to have only one part to its body and is brightly coloured, it is a **WATER MITE**.

65

beaklike jaws for sucking prey

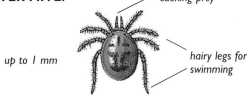

up to 1 mm

hairy legs for swimming

up to 2 mm

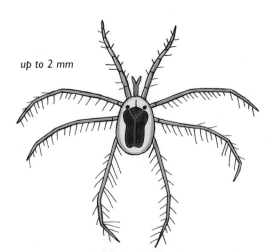

CLUE A If the body of the animal is flattened from side to side, it is a **FRESHWATER SHRIMP.**

 5

CLUE B If the body of the animal is flattened from top to bottom, it is a **WATER SLATER.**

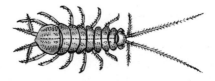

 5

CLUE C If the body of the animal is transparent and flattened from top to bottom, it is probably a **FISH LOUSE.**

 5

CLUE D

If the animal is large and has five pairs of legs, the first pair having long pincers, it is a **FRESHWATER CRAYFISH.**

 58

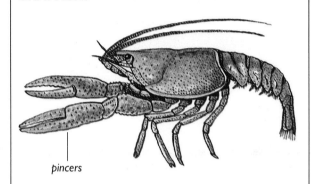

pincers

CLUE E

If the animal is about 20 mm long, transparent, has eleven pairs of leaf-like limbs and swims on its back, it is a **FAIRY SHRIMP.** Fairy shrimps are found in temporary pools or even muddy ruts: their eggs survive drought in dried-up mud.

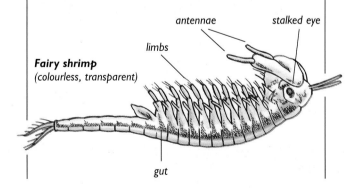

antennae   *stalked eye*

limbs

Fairy shrimp
(colourless, transparent)

gut

For general information on fish, see pages 70–77.

CLUE A   If the fish has a single fin on its back

⇨ 3

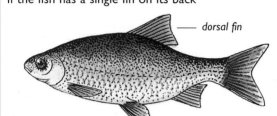

CLUE B   If the fish has two fins on its back

⇨ 3

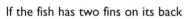

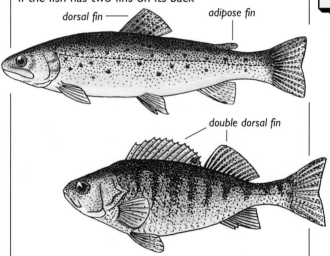

CLUE C   If the fish has a single fin most of the way round its body, it is probably an **EEL.**

⇨ 7

CLUE A

If the fish has six barbels, it may be a **LOACH.**

 73

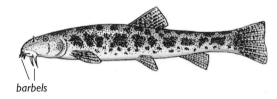

barbels

If the fish has four barbels, it may be a **BARBEL** or **CARP.**

 74, 75

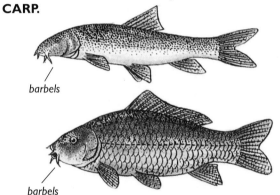

barbels

barbels

If the fish has two barbels, it may be a **GUDGEON** or **TENCH.**

 74

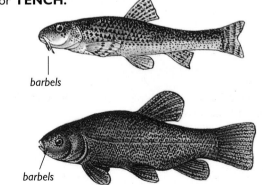

barbels

barbels

CLUE A
continued

If the fish has no barbels and no teeth on its jaws, it may be a **MINNOW, CHUB, DACE** or **RUDD.**

 74, 75

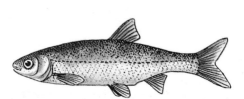

If the fish has no barbels and strong upright teeth in its jaws, it may be a **PIKE.**

 73

CLUE B

If the fish has a large dorsal fin and a small adipose fin, it is a **TROUT.**

 73

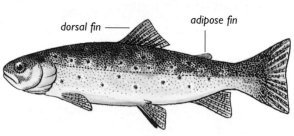

dorsal fin —

adipose fin

CLUE B
continued

If the fish has dorsal fins of similar size, the front one spiny, it is probably a **PERCH**.

 72

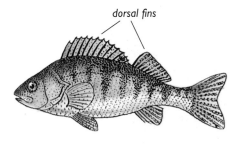

dorsal fins

If the fish has spiny dorsal fins of different sizes and no scales on its body, it is probably a **BULLHEAD**.

 73

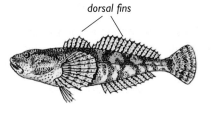

dorsal fins

If the fish has a front dorsal fin with three or ten spines, it is a **STICKLEBACK**.

 72

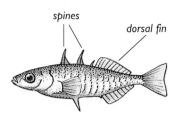

spines   *dorsal fin*

INSECTS – BUGS

Water bugs are most often found in the still water of ponds and the weedy edge of streams. They are all carnivorous and have beak-like jaws for sucking juices from their prey.

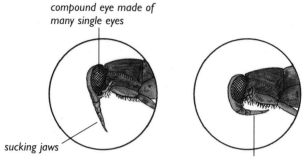

compound eye made of
many single eyes

sucking jaws

jaws tucked under when not in use

Water Boatmen breathe by coming to the surface of the water to collect a bubble of air over their hairy bodies and under their wings. They can stay down only by swimming hard or clinging to plants.

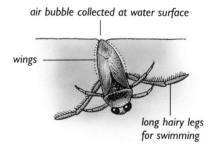

air bubble collected at water surface

wings

long hairy legs
for swimming

The Lesser Water Boatmen scavenge at the bottom of the water.

Water Boatmen may fly from pond to pond during the night.

Water Scorpions are flat animals that live on the bottom at the edge of a pond. They do not fly.

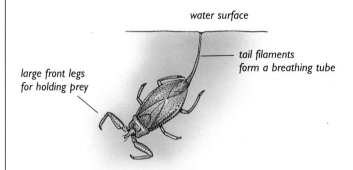

water surface

tail filaments
form a breathing tube

large front legs
for holding prey

Pond Skaters, Water Gnats and Water Crickets skim over the surface of the still water of ponds and the edges of streams. Their bodies have hairs on the underside that keep them dry. Some adult Pond Skaters are wingless. Water Gnats or Water Measurers may also climb plants near the water.

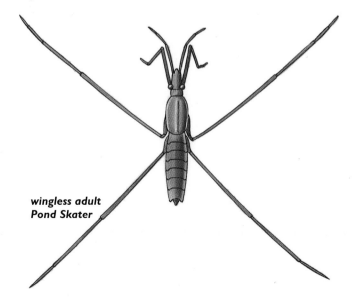

**wingless adult
Pond Skater**

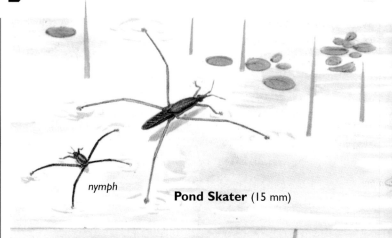

nymph

Pond Skater (15 mm)

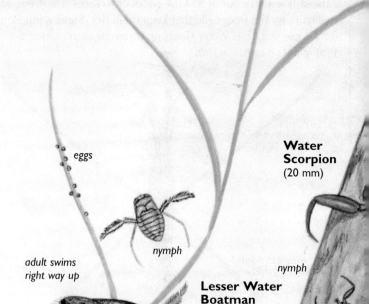

eggs

Water Scorpion (20 mm)

nymph

adult swims right way up

nymph

Lesser Water Boatman (11 mm)

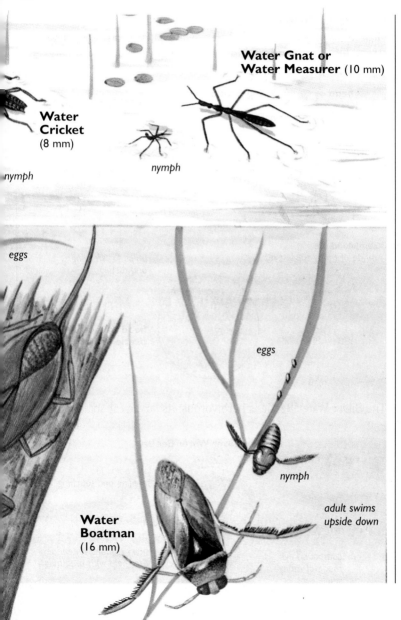

Water Gnat or Water Measurer (10 mm)

Water Cricket (8 mm)

nymph

nymph

nymph

eggs

eggs

Water Boatman (16 mm)

adult swims upside down

Water Beetles most often live in the still water of ponds and ditches. Most kinds of beetles and their larvae are carnivorous; they have strong biting jaws for catching their prey (tadpoles and fish) and sucking the juices.

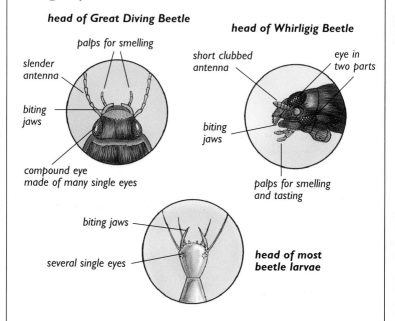

head of Great Diving Beetle

palps for smelling

slender antenna

biting jaws

compound eye made of many single eyes

head of Whirligig Beetle

short clubbed antenna

eye in two parts

biting jaws

palps for smelling and tasting

biting jaws

several single eyes

head of most beetle larvae

The Silver Water Beetle is herbivorous: its larvae eat snails.

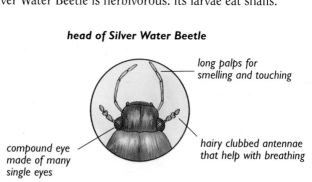

head of Silver Water Beetle

long palps for smelling and touching

compound eye made of many single eyes

hairy clubbed antennae that help with breathing

Most beetles breathe by coming to the surface of the water to collect a bubble of air over their hairy bodies and under their wings.

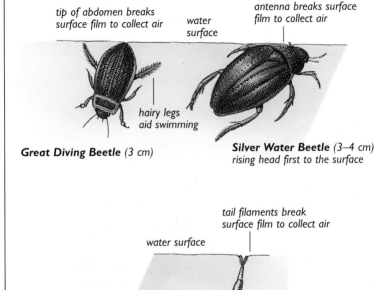

tip of abdomen breaks surface film to collect air

water surface

antenna breaks surface film to collect air

hairy legs aid swimming

Great Diving Beetle *(3 cm)*

Silver Water Beetle *(3–4 cm) rising head first to the surface*

tail filaments break surface film to collect air

water surface

larva of Water Beetle *(25 mm)*

Beetle larvae pupate in damp soil near the water.

The small black beetles that dart and whirl about on the surface are Whirligig Beetles. Screech Beetles squeak when caught.

larva of Screech Beetle *(15 mm)*

tracheal gills for breathing in mud

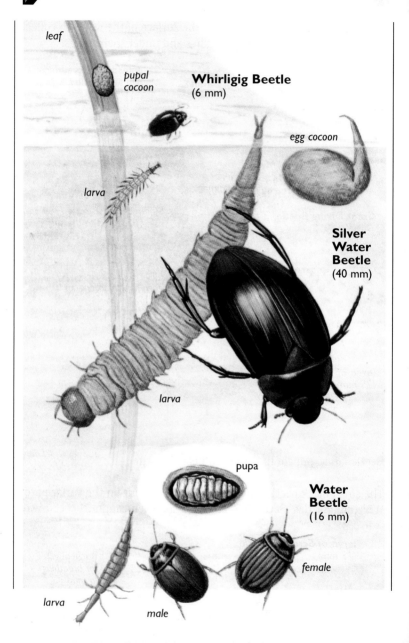

leaf

pupal
cocoon

Whirligig Beetle
(6 mm)

egg cocoon

larva

**Silver
Water
Beetle**
(40 mm)

larva

pupa

**Water
Beetle**
(16 mm)

female

larva

male

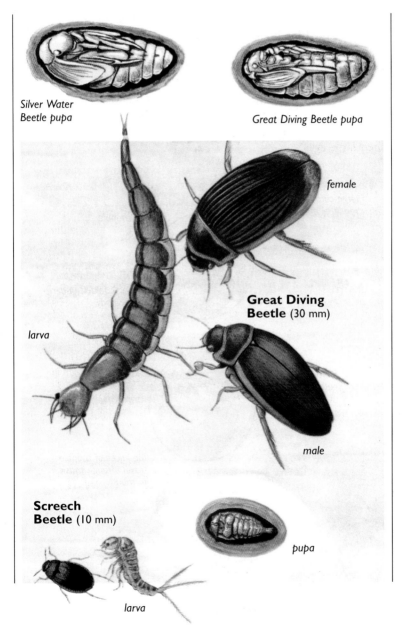

Silver Water Beetle pupa

Great Diving Beetle pupa

female

larva

Great Diving Beetle (30 mm)

male

Screech Beetle (10 mm)

pupa

larva

For the adults of the insects on this page, which do not live in water, see the Clue Book of INSECTS.

DRAGONFLY and DAMSELFLY NYMPHS

Dragonfly and Damselfly nymphs live among the weeds in still water. They are carnivorous and catch animals that come near them by the quick action of their jaws. They see animals coming with their large eyes.

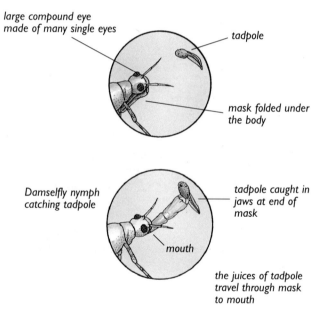

large compound eye made of many single eyes

tadpole

mask folded under the body

Damselfly nymph catching tadpole

tadpole caught in jaws at end of mask

mouth

the juices of tadpole travel through mask to mouth

When nymphs are fully grown (which may take two years) they climb out of the water and cling to the stems of plants. Then the last nymphal case bursts, and the adult emerges. After mating the female drops the eggs singly into the water.

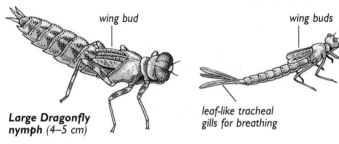

Damselfly nymph (2–3 cm)

wing bud

wing buds

Large Dragonfly nymph (4–5 cm)

leaf-like tracheal gills for breathing

MAYFLY NYMPHS

Mayfly nymphs are scavengers. They live at the bottom of the water. When the nymphs are nearly fully grown they climb out of the water and shed their skins twice more before they become adult. After the first moult they are dull and hairy, and are called 'duns'. Soon after, they shed a second, thin skin and emerge as shiny adults ('spinners'). After mating, most females scatter eggs singly over the water.

Dragonfly, damselfly and mayfly nymphs all breathe below water. Sometimes large dragonfly nymphs move quickly by forcing a jet of water backwards out of their bodies.

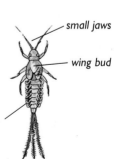

small jaws

wing bud

many tracheal gills for breathing in stagnant water

Mayfly nymph (14 mm)

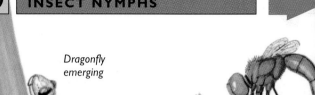

Dragonfly emerging

nymph of **Broad-bodied Dragonfly** (25 mm)

nymph of **Long-bodied Dragonfly** (5 cm)

nymph of **Stonefly** (25 mm)

Mayfly (10 mm)
dun emerging

nymph of
Damselfly (4 cm)

nymph of **Mayfly**
(14 mm)

For the adults of the insects shown on these two pages, which do not live in water, see the Clue Book of **INSECTS**.

ALDERFLY LARVAE (see page 56)

Alderfly larvae are carnivorous. They crawl about in the mud under water for nearly two years. When nearly fully grown the larvae crawl out of the water into damp earth to pupate. After about three weeks the adult flies emerge and mate.

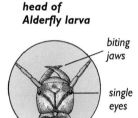

*head of
Alderfly larva*

biting jaws

single eyes

CADDIS LARVAE and PUPAE (see pages 56–57)

Caddis larvae crawl about on the bottom of ponds, lakes and streams, carrying with them a case that covers the soft end of their bodies. Each kind of Caddis larva uses a particular material to make its case. Caddis larvae eat plants.

Caddis larvae spend the winter in water and pupate in their cases in early summer. The pupae cut their way out of the cases and climb out of the water before hatching into adult caddis flies; they mate, and the female lays a mass of eggs.

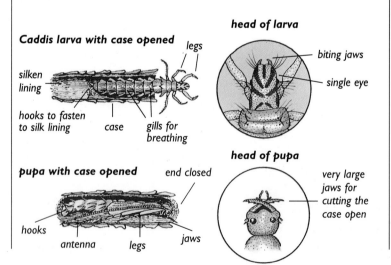

head of larva

Caddis larva with case opened   legs

silken lining

biting jaws

single eye

hooks to fasten to silk lining   case   gills for breathing

head of pupa

pupa with case opened   end closed

very large jaws for cutting the case open

hooks

antenna   legs   jaws

CHINA MARK MOTH CATERPILLARS and PUPAE

China Mark Moth caterpillars live in air-filled tubes under the leaves of water plants. They are herbivorous. They feed by nibbling the leaf round the tube. The caterpillars pupate in the tube.

When the moths emerge they float to the surface of the water, fly away, mate and lay eggs on the underside of leaves in the water.

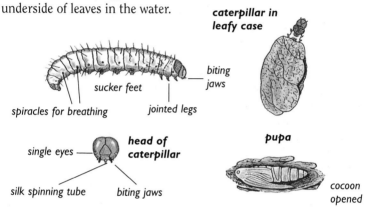

caterpillar in leafy case

biting jaws

sucker feet

spiracles for breathing

jointed legs

single eyes — *head of caterpillar*

silk spinning tube   biting jaws

pupa

cocoon opened

DRONEFLY LARVAE

Droneflies are blackflies that hover 2–3 m high in open spaces. Their larvae scavenge in the mud of stagnant pools. They float to the surface when they change into pupae.

After hatching and mating the females lay clusters of eggs.

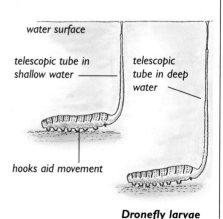

water surface

telescopic tube in shallow water

telescopic tube in deep water

hooks aid movement

Dronefly larvae

For the adults of the insects shown on these two pages, which do not live in water, see the Clue Book of **INSECTS**.
Look carefully at the animals under good magnification.
MOSQUITO (Gnat) and **MIDGE LARVAE** (see page 57) live in still water, including water in rainwater butts and garden pools, and move with quick, wriggling jerks.

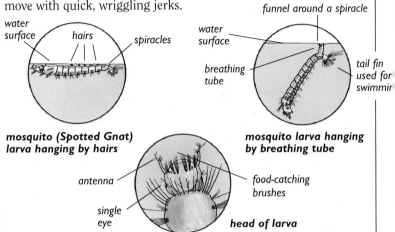

funnel around a spiracle

water surface   *hairs*   *spiracles*

water surface

breathing tube

tail fin used for swimming

mosquito (Spotted Gnat) larva hanging by hairs

mosquito larva hanging by breathing tube

antenna

food-catching brushes

single eye

head of larva

They are scavengers and feed by filtering food from the water through bristles on their heads. Mosquito larvae breathe through holes called **SPIRACLES**, which collect air through the surface film of the water as they hang from it.

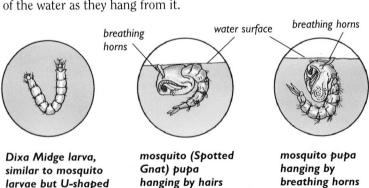

breathing horns

water surface

breathing horns

Dixa Midge larva, similar to mosquito larvae but U-shaped

mosquito (Spotted Gnat) pupa hanging by hairs

mosquito pupa hanging by breathing horns

CHIRONOMUS LARVAE and PUPAE of the HARLEQUIN FLY

Chironomus (non-biting midge) larvae live in tubes in mud or on water plants; they sometimes leave their tubes and move jerkily in the water or scavenge for food in the mud. Some larvae are called **BLOODWORMS** because they are red.

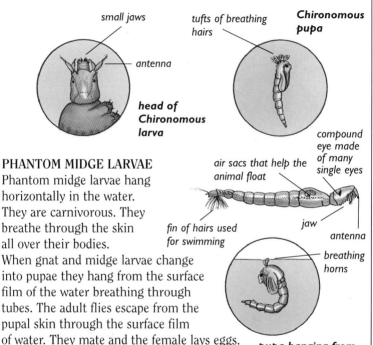

small jaws

antenna

head of Chironomous larva

tufts of breathing hairs

Chironomous pupa

PHANTOM MIDGE LARVAE

Phantom midge larvae hang horizontally in the water. They are carnivorous. They breathe through the skin all over their bodies.

When gnat and midge larvae change into pupae they hang from the surface film of the water breathing through tubes. The adult flies escape from the pupal skin through the surface film of water. They mate and the female lays eggs.

air sacs that help the animal float

compound eye made of many single eyes

fin of hairs used for swimming

jaw

antenna

breathing horns

pupa hanging from surface of water

BLACKFLY LARVAE

Blackfly larvae are common in some fast-flowing streams.

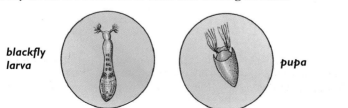

blackfly larva

pupa

cocoon

**China Mark Moth
caterpillar** (20 mm)

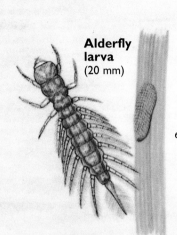

**Alderfly
larva**
(20 mm)

leafy case

eggs

**Caddis larvae in
cases** (10–30 mm)

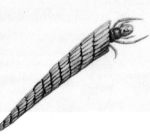

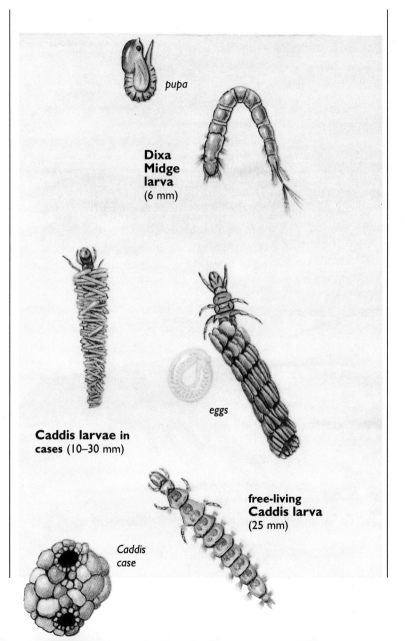

pupa

Dixa Midge larva (6 mm)

Caddis larvae in cases (10–30 mm)

eggs

free-living Caddis larva (25 mm)

Caddis case

Most crustaceans shed their skins (moult) several times as they outgrow them. The new skin hardens after the animal has expanded. During this time damaged legs may also be regrown.

Many female crustaceans carry their eggs and young underneath their bodies, among their legs or swimmerets.

CRAYFISH

Crayfish may be found in streams hiding under stones, or in holes in the banks. They are carnivorous (see page 6) and hunt their prey at night. They are also scavengers (see page 6). Crayfish breathe through gills attached to the tops of their legs under the carapace.

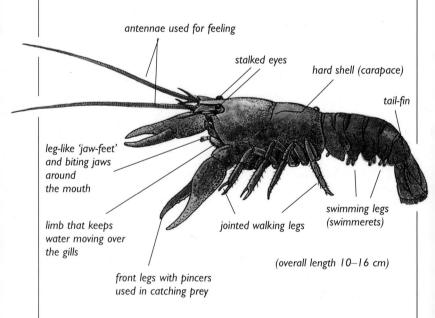

antennae used for feeling

stalked eyes

hard shell (carapace)

tail-fin

leg-like 'jaw-feet' and biting jaws around the mouth

limb that keeps water moving over the gills

jointed walking legs

swimming legs (swimmerets)

front legs with pincers used in catching prey

(overall length 10–16 cm)

FRESHWATER SHRIMPS

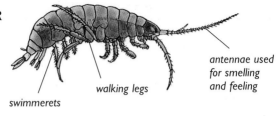

antennae used for smelling and feeling

walking legs

swimmerets

Freshwater shrimps live under stones or in mud in streams and ponds. They swim about on their sides scavenging (see page 6). They breathe through gills attached to the tops of their legs. The females carry their eggs and young among the legs at the front of their bodies.

WATER SLATERS

Water Slaters (Water Lice) live in weedy ponds or streams. Their bodies are flat. They scuttle along scavenging among plants.

antenna used for feeling

small jaws

eggs

jointed legs

underside of Slater

gills for breathing

FISH LICE

Fish Lice are very common parasites on fish. They cling to the fish and suck blood.

sucker used for clinging to fish

compound eye made of many single eyes

flat transparent shell

beak-like jaw for sucking blood

underside of Fish Louse

hairy legs used for swimming

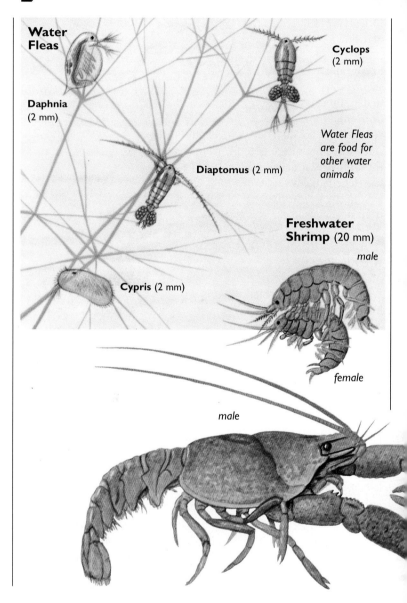

Water Fleas

Daphnia (2 mm)

Cyclops (2 mm)

Diaptomus (2 mm)

Water Fleas are food for other water animals

Cypris (2 mm)

Freshwater Shrimp (20 mm)

male

female

male

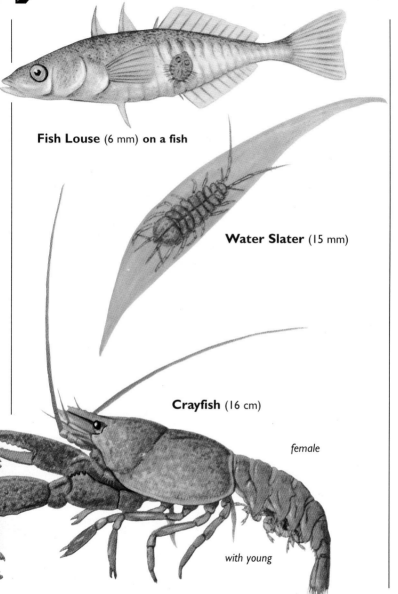

Fish Louse (6 mm) **on a fish**

Water Slater (15 mm)

Crayfish (16 cm)

female

with young

WATER SPIDERS

Water Spiders live in ponds and ditches. They are carnivorous and catch small pond animals which they take back to their webs to suck. Using silk from their spinnerets they build a flat web among water plants which they fill with air by collecting bubbles from the surface of the water and scraping the bubbles off their bodies under the web. When filled with air the web becomes bell-shaped. After mating the female spider adds a new web to the top of the bell and lays her eggs in it. After hatching the young spiders live for some time in the nest before escaping to make their own webs and catch their own food.

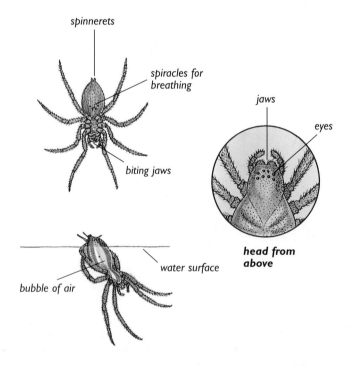

spinnerets

spiracles for breathing

jaws

eyes

biting jaws

head from above

bubble of air

water surface

LEECHES

Leeches live in still and running water. Some leeches cling to other animals, pierce their skin and suck blood.
The small Pond Leech eats insect larvae.
The eggs are most often laid in cocoons (see page 22).

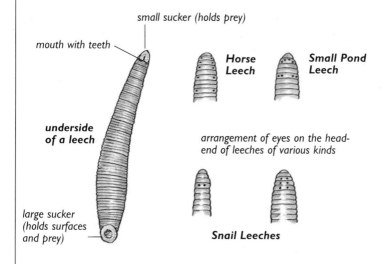

small sucker (holds prey)

mouth with teeth

Horse Leech **Small Pond Leech**

underside of a leech

arrangement of eyes on the head-end of leeches of various kinds

large sucker (holds surfaces and prey)

Snail Leeches

Some snail leeches brood their eggs; the young cling to the adult when they hatch.

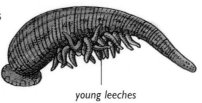

young leeches

WORMS

Worms live in the mud in still and running water. They are scavengers. The eggs are laid in cocoons in the mud (see page 22) and hatch into small worms like their parents.

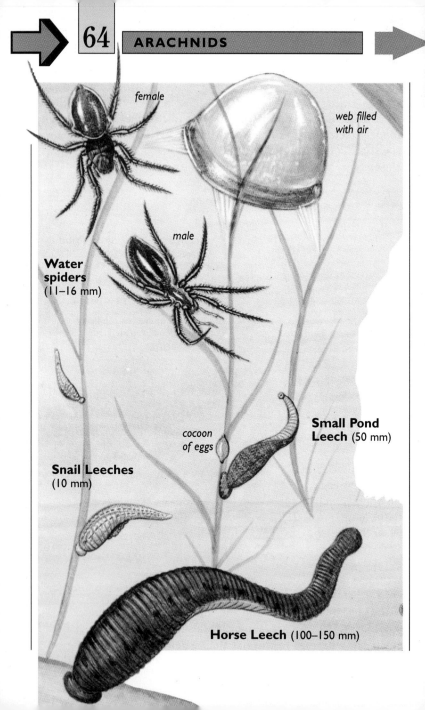

female

web filled with air

male

Water spiders (11–16 mm)

cocoon of eggs

Small Pond Leech (50 mm)

Snail Leeches (10 mm)

Horse Leech (100–150 mm)

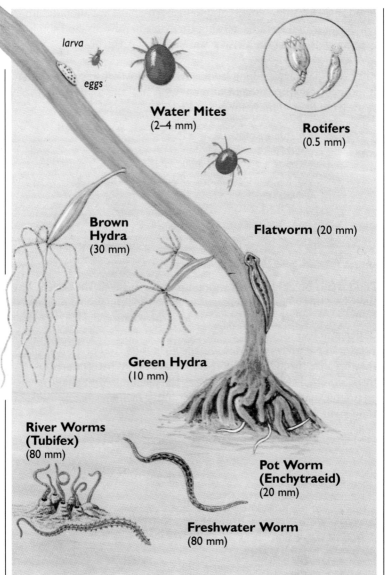

larva

eggs

Water Mites
(2–4 mm)

Rotifers
(0.5 mm)

**Brown
Hydra**
(30 mm)

Flatworm (20 mm)

Green Hydra
(10 mm)

**River Worms
(Tubifex)**
(80 mm)

**Pot Worm
(Enchytraeid)**
(20 mm)

Freshwater Worm
(80 mm)

Pond Snails, Bladder Snails and Ramshorn Snails are all found in ponds, lakes and streams. Most of them are herbivores, and some are scavengers, but the Great Pond Snail is a carnivore.

All these snails have a long tongue, called a **RADULA**, covered with hundreds of teeth. As the front teeth wear out, the tongue and the teeth from behind move forward to take their places.

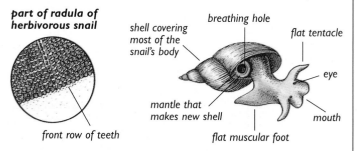

part of radula of herbivorous snail

front row of teeth

shell covering most of the snail's body

breathing hole

flat tentacle

eye

mantle that makes new shell

mouth

flat muscular foot

Pond snails breathe air by coming up to the surface. They open their breathing holes, expel stale air from the lung with a plopping sound, and collect fresh air. They close the opening before returning under water.

Freshwater Winkles and Valve Snails are similar to Pond Snails, but they breathe through gills in their lung cavity. When the snail is inside its shell the operculum closes the opening. Most snails lay eggs after mating, but the eggs of freshwater winkles hatch inside the female's body and appear as live young.

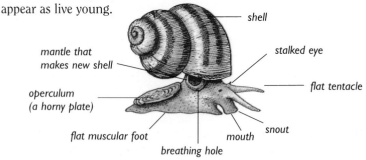

shell

mantle that makes new shell

stalked eye

flat tentacle

operculum (a horny plate)

flat muscular foot

mouth

snout

breathing hole

MUSSELS and COCKLES

Mussels and Cockles have two shells. They move about slowly on a wedge-shaped foot in the mud or sand at the bottom of the water. They feed by siphoning (sucking) water through their bodies. As water is sucked in through the lower siphon it travels over the gills and out of the upper siphon; food is filtered from the water by hair-like cilia on the gills.

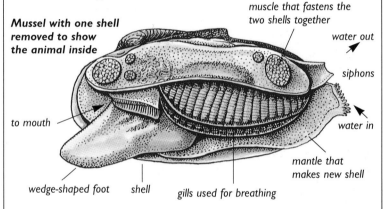

Mussel with one shell removed to show the animal inside

muscle that fastens the two shells together

water out

siphons

to mouth

water in

mantle that makes new shell

wedge-shaped foot   shell   gills used for breathing

The eggs of Freshwater Mussels hatch into larvae among the gills of female mussels. The larvae pass out through the upper siphon and attach themselves to fish, on which they feed until they become young mussels.

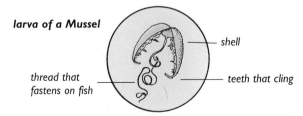

larva of a Mussel

shell

thread that fastens on fish

teeth that cling

The eggs of Cockles hatch among the gills of the females into young like their parents, and pass out through the upper siphon.

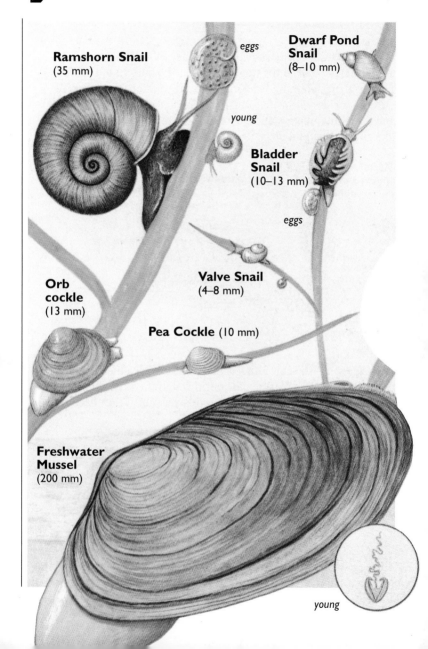

Ramshorn Snail (35 mm)

eggs

Dwarf Pond Snail (8–10 mm)

young

Bladder Snail (10–13 mm)

eggs

Orb cockle (13 mm)

Valve Snail (4–8 mm)

Pea Cockle (10 mm)

Freshwater Mussel (200 mm)

young

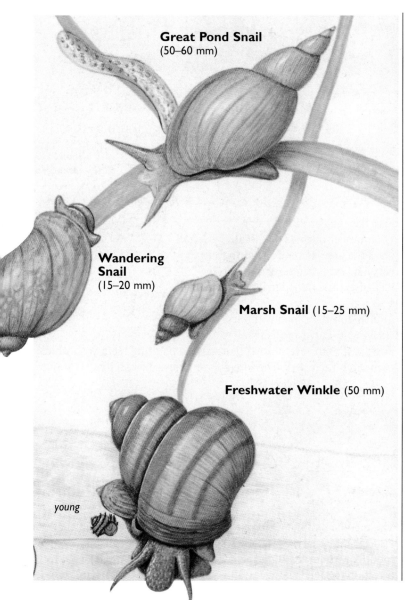

Great Pond Snail (50–60 mm)

Wandering Snail (15–20 mm)

Marsh Snail (15–25 mm)

Freshwater Winkle (50 mm)

young

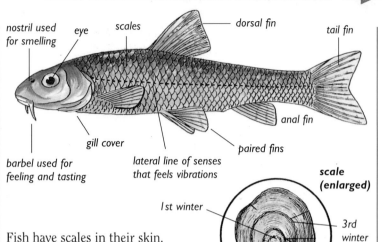

nostril used for smelling • eye • scales • dorsal fin • tail fin • anal fin • paired fins • lateral line of senses that feels vibrations • gill cover • barbel used for feeling and tasting

scale (enlarged)

1st winter • 3rd winter • 2nd winter

in winter growth rings are close together showing little growth

Fish have scales in their skin. The number of rings on a scale gives the approximate age of the fish. The rings can be counted if looked at under good magnification.

All fish bolt their food without chewing it. Carnivorous fish have large jaws with several rows of backward pointing teeth with which they catch their prey. These teeth are renewed when they wear out.

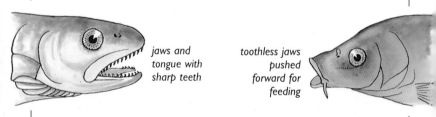

jaws and tongue with sharp teeth

toothless jaws pushed forward for feeding

The members of the CARP family most often eat plants, but they also eat insect larvae and other small animals. These fish have small mouths without teeth on the jaws. Teeth in their throats begin to break up the food as they swallow it.

Fish breathe by taking oxygen from the water. As a fish opens and closes its mouth it takes in water, but instead of swallowing it, it pushes the water over the gills and out under the gill covers.

head of fish with the gill cover removed

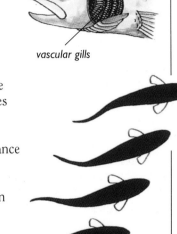

vascular gills

Most fish can move easily through water because they are streamlined. The curving movements that push the fish along are produced by the muscles (flesh) in the body and tail.

Body and tail fins help the fish to balance and change direction.

Freshwater fish most often lay eggs on sand or gravel in still water. Male Sticklebacks and Bullheads make nests in which the females lay eggs. The eggs are fertilized by sperm (milt) from the male after the female has laid them.

male Stickleback fanning with its fins to aerate the eggs

stone

male guarding and aerating the eggs

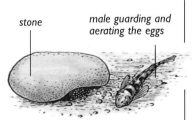

nest of Stickleback

Bullhead eggs attached to a stone

Eels swim out to sea to lay their eggs and then die. The young, called elvers, swim back to the rivers in the spring.

MAINLY MEAT-EATING

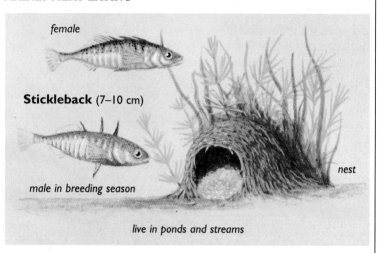

female

Stickleback (7–10 cm)

male in breeding season

nest

live in ponds and streams

Perch (15–45 cm)

live in lakes, ponds and rivers

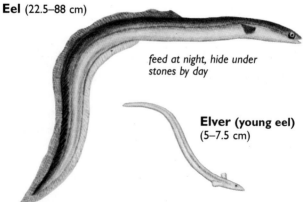

Eel (22.5–88 cm)

feed at night, hide under stones by day

Elver (young eel) (5–7.5 cm)

Loach (10–14 cm)

live at the bottom of streams, but sometimes come to the surface to gulp air

Bullhead
(10–17.5 cm)

live at the bottom or under stones in clear streams

Trout
(18–57 cm)

live in clear running water

Pike (Water Wolf)
(37–100 cm)

live in deep holes in the slow- running water of lakes, ponds and rivers

MAINLY PLANT-EATING

live in clear streams

Minnow (7.5–10 cm)

Gudgeon (10–14 cm)

Dace (15–25 cm)

live in the shallow water of rivers, moving about in shoals

live in clear running water

Tench (18–60 cm)

live in pools and slow-running muddy water

Carp (38–70 cm)

live in ponds and slow-running muddy water

Goldfish (8–20 cm)

live in garden pools

Rudd (15–30 cm)

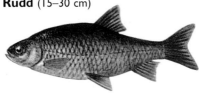

live in slow-running weedy water

Roach (12.5–30 cm)

live in slow-running water

Chub (27–57 cm)

live near the surface of running water

Barbel (30–80 cm)

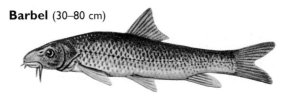

live in rivers

Frogs, toads and newts are AMPHIBIANS. They are always found in damp places. They often hide in holes or under stones in the daytime and move about at night. In spring they return to the water for a short time to mate and lay eggs. Adults breathe through their moist skin, and also gulp air through their mouths. Watch the movements of their throats as they push the air into their lungs.

Amphibians are carnivorous. They catch flies, small worms and other small animals by flicking out their long tongues.

Amphibians sometimes shed their skins.

A frog's colouring becomes lighter or darker to match its surroundings.

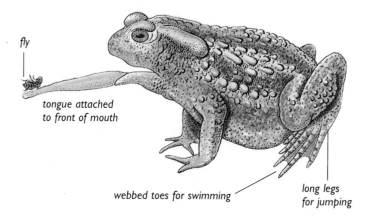

fly

tongue attached to front of mouth

webbed toes for swimming

long legs for jumping

The male frog has large thumb pads on his front legs which help him to cling to the female's back while fertilizing the eggs she lays.

thumb pad of male frog

FROG and TOAD LIFE CYCLE

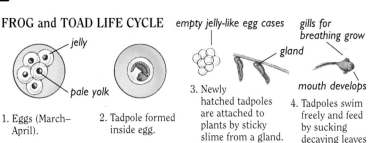

jelly

pale yolk

1. Eggs (March–April).

2. Tadpole formed inside egg.

empty jelly-like egg cases

gland

3. Newly hatched tadpoles are attached to plants by sticky slime from a gland.

gills for breathing grow

mouth develops

4. Tadpoles swim freely and feed by sucking decaying leaves and stems.

surface of water

— *jaws*

back leg

— *front leg*

5. Jaws with horny teeth grow and the tadpole begins to eat small animals as well as plants. A flap of skin grows back over the gills.

6. Back legs begin to grow.

7. Front legs appear.

8. Tail disappears and the small frog or toad leaves the water (June–July).

Tadpoles come to the surface to breathe air through their mouths when their lungs grow.

NEWT LIFE CYCLE
Newt tadpoles feed on water fleas and very small worms.

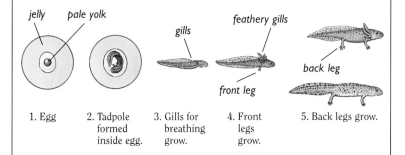

jelly *pale yolk*

gills

feathery gills

back leg

front leg

1. Egg

2. Tadpole formed inside egg.

3. Gills for breathing grow.

4. Front legs grow.

5. Back legs grow.

When the gills have been replaced by lungs the young newts leave the water (mid-August).

Common Frog (4–8 cm)

tadpole

eggs (spawn)

tadpole

egg

Common Newt (6–8 cm)

egg

tadpole

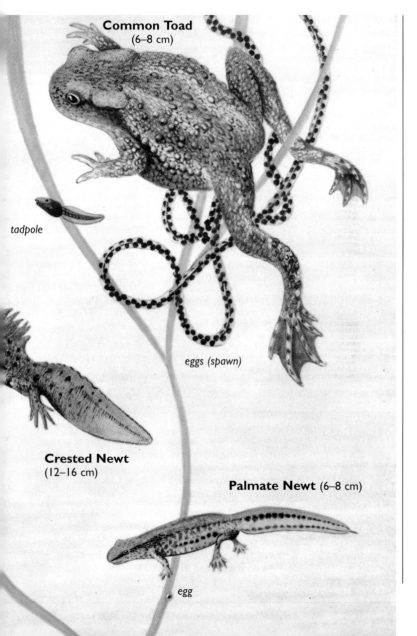

Common Toad
(6–8 cm)

tadpole

eggs (spawn)

Crested Newt
(12–16 cm)

Palmate Newt (6–8 cm)

egg

L125,089 JNP591

Further Reading

Amphibians. Eyewitness Series, Dorling Kindersley, 1989.
Parker, Steve, *Fish.* Eyewitness Series, Dorling Kindersley, 1990.
Ganeri, Anita, *Rivers, Ponds and Lakes.* Ecology Watch Series, Cloverleaf, 1991.
Parker, Steve, *Pond and River.* Eyewitness Series, Dorling Kindersley, 1988.

A good way to learn more about the animals and plants in your area is to join Wildlife Watch, a club for young people interested in wildlife and the environment. As well as organising activities for its members, Watch produces a national magazine, local newsletters, and many posters and activity packs. Their address is Wildlife Watch, The Green, Witham Park, Waterside South, Lincoln LN5 7JR.